Who Was Katherine Johnson?

by Shelia P. Moses

illustrated by Dede Putra

Penguin Workshop

Ms. Rosetta Adams taught my mother in the early
1940s. She was my teacher in the late 1970s.
This book is dedicated to you, Ms. Adams.
One of my sheroes!—SPM

PENGUIN WORKSHOP
An imprint of Penguin Random House LLC
1745 Broadway, New York, New York 10019

First published in the United States of America by Penguin Workshop,
an imprint of Penguin Random House LLC, New York, 2025

Visit us online at penguinrandomhouse.com.

Library of Congress Cataloging-in-Publication Data is available.

Printed in the United States of America

ISBN 9780593752166 (paperback)   10 9 8 7 6 5 4 3 2   CJKW
ISBN 9780593752173 (library binding)   10 9 8 7 6 5 4 3 2 1 CJKW

The authorized representative in the EU for product safety and compliance is
Penguin Random House Ireland, Morrison Chambers, 32 Nassau Street,
Dublin D02 YH68, Ireland, https://eu-contact.penguin.ie.

Contents

Who Was Katherine Johnson?

On July 20, 1969, like millions of other Americans, Katherine Johnson was excitedly staring at a television screen. But she wasn't just any viewer—she was a brilliant mathematician who played a key role in what was about to happen.

Katherine worked at the National Aeronautics and Space Administration (NASA), the place where space missions are planned. Astronaut Neil Armstrong and his crew had launched into space several days before and were heading for the moon. Katherine and her colleagues had done tons of calculations to ensure the mission would be a success. If everything went correctly, the United States would be the first country to put a person on the moon! As the rocket roared into the sky, Katherine hurried to join her sorority sisters from Alpha Kappa Alpha who were gathered at a hotel in the Poconos, Pennsylvania, for a convention.

When the lunar module, called the *Eagle*, landed on the moon, everyone held their breath.

The *Eagle* lands on the moon

Then, over the speakers, they heard Neil say, "The *Eagle* has landed." The room instantly became filled with cheers and happy screams. Katherine and her sorority sisters couldn't believe it—they had just witnessed history!

At 10:56 p.m. EST (Eastern Standard Time, the time zone that covers the eastern part of the United States, Canada, and parts of the Caribbean and Central America), the whole world watched as Neil took his first steps on the moon, saying,

"That's one small step for man, one giant leap for mankind." Katherine knew that behind that giant leap was a lot of hard work from Black mathematicians like her.

Katherine wasn't just proud of the moon landing. She was proud of her part in it. She once said, "We were the pioneers of the space era," and pointed out that "everything is physics and math," reminding future scientists that the universe is full of numbers just waiting to be discovered.

After the mission, the news of this incredible achievement spread across the nation and the world. On July 24, 1969, at 12:50 p.m. EST, Neil and his fellow astronauts splashed down safely into the Pacific Ocean, not far from Honolulu, Hawaii. They were back home, and so was Katherine, both eventually becoming celebrated as American heroes.

Neil Armstrong and other astronauts splash down
into the Pacific Ocean

CHAPTER 1
A Curious Childhood

Katherine Coleman was born to Joylette Roberta Lowe and Joshua Coleman. Joylette, who grew up in Danville, Virginia, suffered from serious allergies as a young girl, so at age eighteen, she moved to White Sulphur Springs, West Virginia. She hoped the new city would bring great job opportunities and cleaner air. Not only did she find a job as a schoolteacher, but she also met a tall, handsome man named Joshua Coleman.

Joshua—who always wore a stylish Stetson hat—got a lot of attention from the women in town, who thought he was a good catch, but he only had eyes for Joylette. They dated for a few years and got married in 1909. The young couple moved into Joshua's log cabin on the farm he had inherited, just seven miles outside White Sulphur Springs in an area called Dutch Run. Joylette loved teaching, but she stopped in 1912 when she gave birth to their first child, a son named Horace. Two years later, they had their first daughter, Margaret, followed by another son, Charlie. Katherine, who was born in 1918, would be the couple's last child.

Joshua was a great provider who worked as a farmer and horseman, and he could build anything, including houses. He was so naturally good with numbers that he didn't use a measuring tape when he was building. He could look at the construction plans and determine the amount of

wood that was needed. And he shared his love
of numbers with his children.

The Colemans were very happy living on the
farm, but they wanted to give the kids a chance
to learn with other students. They knew Joylette
could not teach the children at home forever.

So around 1922, the family moved to White Sulphur Springs and Joshua built them a big white house in town. They loved their new home, which had running water and a bathroom.

White Sulphur Springs

Joshua found a good job at the Greenbriar Hotel while Joylette took care of the chores in the house. She also taught Katherine when the older siblings attended White Sulphur Grade School. Much like her father, Katherine was very smart and very good with numbers. She walked from room to room in their house counting everything because she was so eager to learn. If Katherine's mother turned her back for one minute, Katherine would sneak out of the house and go to the two-room school. Joylette would find Katherine sitting beside one of her siblings in class with a big smile on her face.

But as the Coleman children got older, they were faced with a problem. Once they finished grade school, they would not have a high school to attend. Katherine's parents wanted their kids to have the same opportunities as other children, so they sent Horace and Margaret to the town of Institute, West Virginia, to attend West Virginia Collegiate Institute. The school was founded in 1891 as a high school for Black

students that also provided vocational and teacher training, but it started offering college degrees in 1915. The Coleman children now had the opportunity to attend high school and college.

But why was it so difficult for Katherine and her siblings to go to school?

The school was 127 miles from White Sulphur Springs, and the Colemans were not happy to be so far away from their older children.

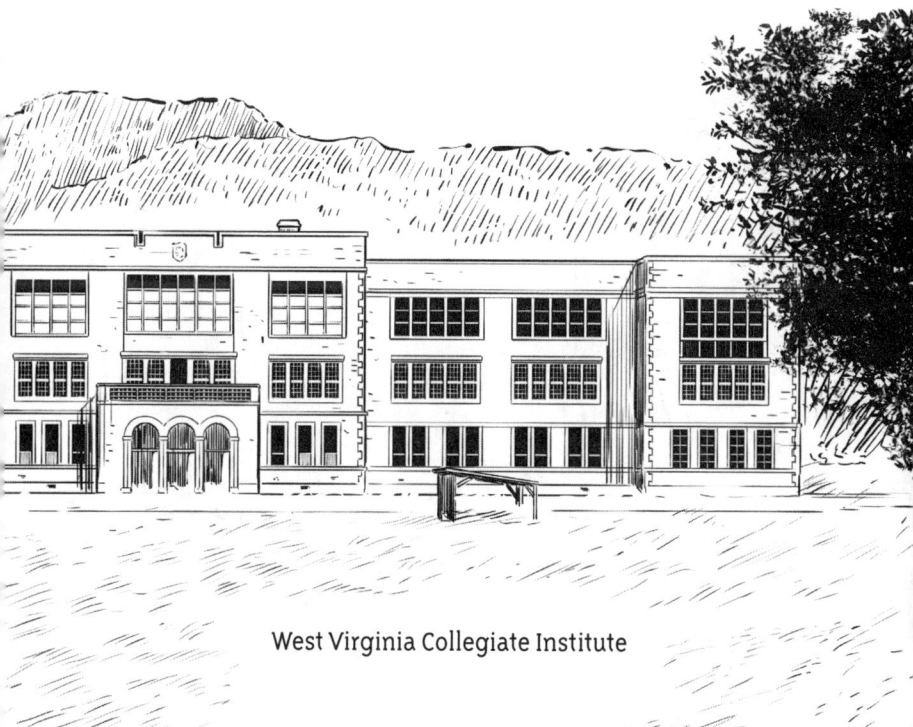

West Virginia Collegiate Institute

When it was time for Charlie to leave, the Colemans made another hard decision. Joshua decided to sell his family's farm in Dutch Run so they would have money for the entire family to move to Institute.

Dr. John Warren Davis

When they arrived in Institute, they lived with Joylette's cousin for a little while and eventually rented a house directly across the street from campus. The Colemans loved being near all their children. They were happy to know that their children would be attending West Virginia Collegiate Institute, which was renamed West Virginia State in 1929 under the leadership of their new president, Dr. John Warren Davis.

Katherine's older siblings were all enrolled in high school; she enrolled in the primary school nearby, where she was an excellent student.

Joshua soon realized that he would have to move back to the big white house in White Sulphur Springs because he could not find a job in Institute that paid enough to cover their bills and school tuition. They also wanted to save money for their children to go to college. Joshua missed his family, so he traveled back to Institute on weekends whenever he could.

To earn extra money to help the family, Joylette and Margaret started ironing clothes for white people attending the institute. Horace and Charlie got a newspaper route and delivered milk. Little Katherine was too young to work, so she wrote letters to their father to tell him everything that was going on in Institute.

It was a difficult time for the family, but their hard work was paying off. They were smart children. Katherine was so smart that as the years passed, the principal let her skip first grade. She also skipped seventh grade. When Katherine was only ten years old, she started high school.

Katherine was very active in high school. As she approached her teen years, she spent more time on campus, even after school. She learned to play tennis and started taking piano and French lessons.

Her math teacher, Mrs. Evans, noticed how good she was with numbers and took a special interest in Katherine. Mrs. Evans, who was married to the head of the college's math department, Dr. James Evans, often invited Katherine and her friend Constance Davis, who Katherine called Dit, over for tea. Constance and her sister Dorothy were the daughters of the college's president.

By Katherine's senior year, all of her teachers were encouraging her to focus on math and become a math teacher. At fifteen years old, she graduated from high school.

CHAPTER 2
Welcome to College

During the summer of 1936, as Katherine prepared to start college, the Colemans went back to White Sulphur Springs to work at the Greenbriar Hotel with Joshua for two months. The Great Depression was affecting the entire country; the Colemans were struggling financially no matter how hard they worked. The boys worked as bellhops. Margaret and Katherine worked in valet services.

The Greenbriar Hotel

One day while Katherine was at work, a white woman who called herself Countess Sara was speaking French and noticed that Katherine understood her. She was so impressed that a Black girl knew French that she asked the Parisian chef at the Greenbriar Hotel to work with Katherine to improve her second language.

Katherine was happy because she realized that she was mastering French and math and was also very good in music.

When Katherine returned to Institute that

fall, she was so excited to start college. She loved to roller-skate, and she used her skates to get around campus daily. On the weekends, she joined her friends on a hill nearby to skate, and they had a great time.

Katherine enjoyed the extra activities on campus, but she was very focused on her classes. A former math teacher at her school, Mrs. Lacey, had returned, and she encouraged Katherine to become a math teacher, along with another math professor named Dr. William Claytor. One day he stopped at Katherine's desk and said, "You know, you would make a good research mathematician."

Katherine had never heard the term, so she asked him what it meant.

"You do research in math." He chuckled. He could see what she could not see for her future. Not yet!

Dr. William Claytor, mathematician

During her sophomore year of college, Katherine joined the sorority Alpha Kappa Alpha, learned to hike with her classmates, and continued to take piano lessons. She was so excited and wanted to learn as much as possible about different areas of life. She learned from her instructors and the guest speakers who came to campus, such as entertainers Paul Robeson and Marian Anderson. Yes, they were entertainers, but they were also civil rights activists long before the movement started and before Dr. Martin Luther King Jr. was even out of elementary school.

Paul Robeson

Marian Anderson

Katherine did so well in school that she received a scholarship her last year in college that included room and board on campus. She moved to campus, and her mother moved back to White Sulphur Springs to live full-time for the first time in over a decade.

During Katherine's senior year, Dr. Claytor created a course called Analytic Geometry of Space just for her. No one else wanted to take it, so Dr. Claytor would teach her daily as if the class were full of students. He kept teaching, and she kept learning.

Divine Nine

The "Divine Nine" is a group of nine historically Black Greek-letter fraternities and sororities. They were first created in the early twentieth century because Black college students were not allowed to join the Greek organizations that existed on college campuses for white students. This was one way for Black students to connect with each other and build support networks. Each group has its own unique history, traditions, and symbols, but they all focus on uplifting the Black community and helping people.

THE FRATERNITIES

- Alpha Phi Alpha Fraternity, Inc. (founded in 1906)
- Kappa Alpha Psi Fraternity, Inc. (founded in 1911)
- Omega Psi Phi Fraternity, Inc. (founded in 1911)
- Phi Beta Sigma Fraternity, Inc. (founded in 1914)
- Iota Phi Theta Fraternity, Inc. (founded in 1963)

The Alpha Kappa Alpha logo

THE SORORITIES

- **Alpha Kappa Alpha Sorority, Inc. (founded in 1908)**

- **Delta Sigma Theta Sorority, Inc. (founded in 1913)**

- **Zeta Phi Beta Sorority, Inc. (founded in 1920)**

- **Sigma Gamma Rho Sorority, Inc. (founded in 1922)**

Katherine's parents wanted her to become a math teacher, and she believed she could go as far as being a professor. Dr. Claytor believed she could become a research mathematician.

In the spring of 1937, Katherine graduated summa cum laude with a degree in math and French. The Coleman family was so proud.

CHAPTER 3
The Student Becomes the Teacher

After graduation, Katherine returned home to live with her parents while she looked for a job. It was not easy for a college-educated Black woman to find work, but Katherine was determined. Finally, in early August 1937, she received a letter from Carnegie Elementary School in Marion,

Virginia, offering her a job under one condition: They were only interested if she could play the piano. Of course, she could play the piano, and she was on her way to Marion to teach fourth through sixth graders French, math, and music!

In late August, Katherine got on the back of the bus, where all Black people had to sit, and headed to a new city to start her first job, other than working with her parents at the hotel. Her parents warned her to be careful on the three-hour bus trip; she was going deeper into the South and deeper into segregation. The moment they crossed the Virginia state line, the bus driver came to an immediate stop. "All Negroes to the back!" he shouted. When she arrived in Marion, the bus driver stopped several miles from the Black neighborhood. But the Black taxi drivers knew this always happened, so they waited close by each time a bus arrived.

Katherine hopped in a taxi that took her to the principal's house first, where she got the information for school and the address for his friend who would be renting Katherine a room. She was happy to find a pleasant home with Mrs. Gert Ross, who was known as Aunt Gert. Aunt Gert lived in an area known as Up the Creek because a small creek literally ran through the neighborhood. On her fifty-dollars-a-month salary, Katherine would have to adjust to living with a stranger because that was all she could afford.

Reverend Amos Carnegie

She enjoyed teaching at the two-story brick school that had only four classrooms. Carnegie was small but the pride of the community; it was named after Reverend Amos Carnegie after he wrote a grant to get a school built for the Black children in Marion in 1931. Katherine also enjoyed creating school plays for the children to participate in, and she would always invite people in the community to attend. This grew into a local event that included plays and comedy shows.

Katherine had been in Marion only a few months before meeting one of her students' older brothers, Jimmie, who volunteered to be in one of her plays. Jimmie Goble was one of thirteen children in this musical family.

Jimmie Goble

"Do you know the song 'I Love You Truly'?" Katherine asked him at auditions.

"Why, Miss Coleman, you don't know me well enough to say that to me," Jimmie joked with the new teacher. They became friends, and before they knew it, they were a couple. Katherine enjoyed spending time with Jimmie and his family. She also felt safe with Jimmie and his family because out of five thousand people living in Marion, 96 percent were white.

Katherine understood racism very well, so she and Jimmie were careful about what they did and where they went. The young couple was very much in love.

CHAPTER 4
Breaking Barriers

In 1939, Katherine and Jimmie got married in her hometown. Her parents did attend the wedding, but her father was not happy about the union.

Joshua didn't give Katherine a good reason why he didn't want her to get married. Katherine was puzzled because they all knew Jimmie was a great man and from a nice family. She wondered if her father was concerned about her keeping her job if she got married. In many states,

female schoolteachers could not continue to teach if they got married. Principals feared they would start having children and would miss too much time from work. Keeping her father's concerns in mind, Katherine and Jimmie got married quietly at the big white house so that Katherine could continue to teach.

After the wedding, Jimmie went back to Marion to teach school, but Katherine stayed in White Sulphur Springs because she received a job offer paying $110 per month to teach in the neighboring town of Morgantown. This also kept people from knowing they were married.

One day after class, she was shocked to see her former college president, Dr. Davis, and his colleague Dr. Evans, waiting to talk to her. They had great news for Katherine.

She had a chance to go to West Virginia University in Morgantown as one of the first three Black students in their graduate program. She was the only woman. Not only was she offered a chance to attend the school, but she had free room and board near campus. Her mother moved with her to Morgantown so that she would not be alone. This was the opportunity Katherine had been waiting for: a chance to advance to one day become a professor at a college or a research mathematician, as Dr. Claytor had mentioned years ago.

Katherine was in Morgantown only a few months before she realized she would not be able to finish the program, as she was pregnant with her first child. Jimmie and Katherine were very happy, but Dr. Davis and Dr. Evans were disappointed that she was moving back to Marion.

Katherine went to be with her husband but was worried the entire time she was pregnant because Black and white men were being drafted daily to potentially fight in World War II. Both of her brothers were already in the service, but Jimmie failed his physical when he was finally called. Like all Americans, Katherine's family was devastated when the Japanese attacked Pearl Harbor on December 7, 1941, the start of America's involvement in World War II.

Pearl Harbor attack

Katherine and Jimmie's first daughter, Joylette, who they named after Katherine's mother, was born in 1940. They would eventually have two more daughters, Connie and Katherine, who they adored.

Even though the Great Depression was over, the young family still struggled to make ends meet. During the summer, they would pack their bags and spend a few weeks in Rocky Mount, North Carolina, working for a wealthy white family, the Belchers, who owned a lumber company. The family was nice to the Gobles, but they were always reminded that the color of their skin mattered. One day Mr. Belcher was showing Joylette how to horseback ride when she was thrown from the horse. Mr. Belcher took her to the hospital, but she was not allowed entrance because she was Black. Katherine and Jimmie dreamed of and worked hard for the day their children's skin color would not matter.

With hopes of not always having to work for white people in the summers, Jimmie took a job as a teacher and coach in Bluefield, West Virginia. Katherine was happy about the move because she was closer to her family. They eventually rented a small apartment in the Carson mansion in Bluefield and enrolled the girls in the school where Katherine was now teaching.

It was a house that was once owned by a white family. The Carsons, who were Black, had purchased the home and converted it into a boardinghouse.

In 1950, the Colemans' joy faded when two tragedies happened the same year. They were so sad when Katherine's brother Horace fell ill and was

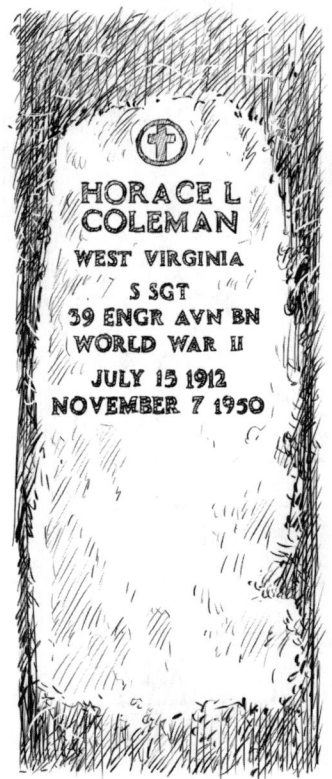

diagnosed with leukemia. Like thousands of soldiers who came home from World War II with some form of cancer, he died young and left them and his wife brokenhearted. Many believe he got cancer from the radiation while at war. After his death, Katherine tried to get back to normal for the sake of the children.

What seemed to be a normal life changed again when she was at a wedding reception with Jimmie and heard someone say there was a fire at the Carson mansion. They ran down the street to find the side of the house where they lived up in flames. They screamed for the girls as the neighbors tried to help. Someone finally told them that their girls were safe next door.

Jimmie's football players had rushed into the house and gotten the girls out with no burns but a little smoke inhalation.

Katherine and Jimmie took their daughters and the few things that didn't burn and went to live with her parents. Her mother pulled out the sewing machine and started making clothes

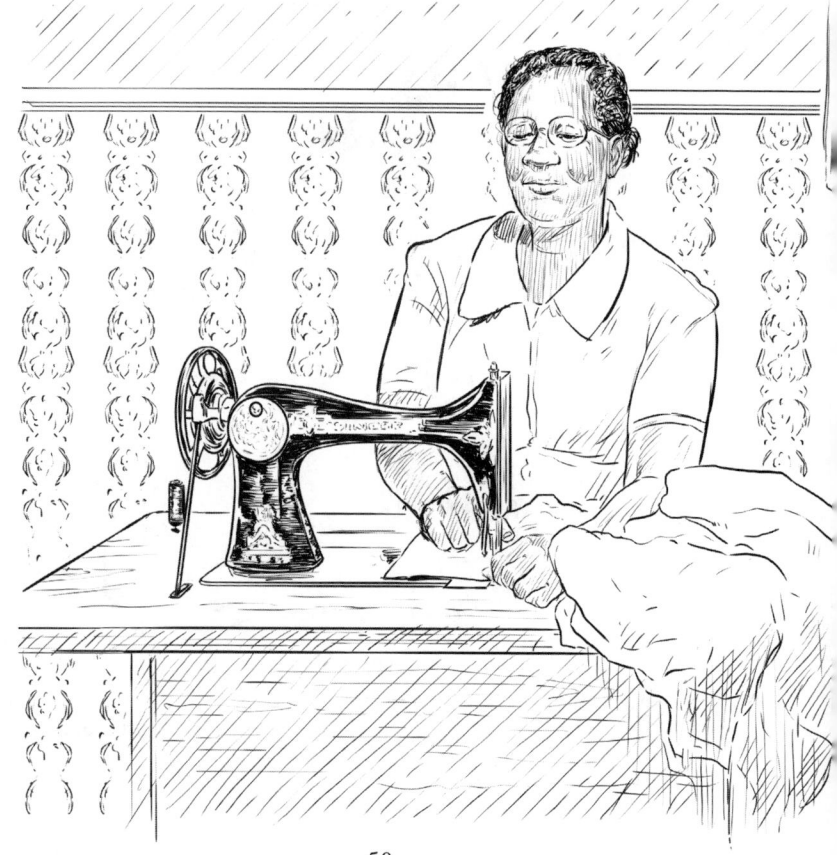

for the girls and Katherine. Once Jimmie and Katherine knew for sure the girls had recovered from smoke inhalation, they decided to return to Bluefield. This time they rented out a room and left the girls behind with their grandparents to finish the school year.

CHAPTER 5
Welcome to NASA

In the summer of 1952, while in Marion for a family wedding, Jimmie's sister Margaret and brother-in-law Eric invited him and Katherine to come live in Newport News, Virginia. Eric was very well known in the area and promised to help them get higher-paying jobs. Eric told Katherine about a federal agency in the Hampton Roads area that was hiring Black women with degrees in math to work at the National Advisory Committee for Aeronautics (NACA), which later became NASA.

He also told them about an area near Hampton Roads where Black families rented trailer homes. Hampton Roads was an area that connected three cities: Norfolk, Virginia Beach, and Chesapeake. This area was also called the Peninsula.

Jimmie and Katherine were not sure about moving the girls again, but they knew that moving to Newport News meant more money to help them pay for their daughters' college education. They had never owned their own house, and this was their chance. Jimmie and Katherine went back to Bluefield, resigned from their jobs, packed the few things they had left after the fire, and went off to start a new life in Hampton Roads.

The girls were happy as they got closer to Virginia and saw lots of cars, fewer trees, and more buildings. It was their first time living in a larger city.

Newport News, Virginia

Jimmie got a job as a painter at the shipyard and made a lot more money than his teaching salary. Because he was educated, he was quickly promoted to supervisor and became active in the union. Katherine took a position as a substitute teacher.

One day Eric told her he needed her to meet a woman who had been with NACA since 1943 and was the first Black supervisor. To Katherine's surprise, the woman was Dorothy Vaughan, who she had met years earlier in West Virginia.

Dorothy Vaughan

There were no computers like we see today, so people did math on paper and were considered human computers.

Dorothy told Katherine that she didn't have any positions at the time but to put in her application. Katherine applied for the job, and then she waited. The next day, in May 1953, she was offered a job at NACA, the same day the principal at her school offered her a full-time job.

Katherine loved teaching, but she knew she had to decline the teaching position and take the position with NACA. She knew that she and

Jimmie would have to leave education to earn more money. They had no choice.

In June 1953, Katherine was on her way to work at NACA as a human computer. The family had only one car, so Katherine rode to work with fellow church member and sorority sister Eunice Smith, who was also a human computer.

Eunice Smith

Eunice was so smart that NACA had hired her fresh out of college at Hampton Institute.

Katherine was very excited when she arrived at Langley Field to fill out her paperwork in human resources and pick up her badge. She proudly pinned her badge on her white blouse and reported to the Aircraft Loads building. Dorothy, who they called Mrs. Vaughan at work, supervised Katherine as well as around twenty-four other Black women.

Katherine was doing an excellent job and had been at work for only two weeks when she was called into a meeting by Mrs. Vaughan along with another employee named Erma Walker. The women were shocked when they learned that they both were being transferred to the Flight Research Division to work as human computers. This was big news because the Flight Research department was the most important area of NACA. Their mission was to research and design aircraft as America entered a race with Russia to have the first man in space. Katherine packed up her desk and was off to Building 1244.

Katherine felt ready for the job her former professor Dr. Claytor had told her she could have one day. She was now a math researcher. The division chief was a white man named Henry Pearson. Katherine was responsible for researching aircraft safety issues; she was good at her job.

The white men refused to talk to her, and she wasn't allowed to attend any meetings. Katherine knew that she had no time to complain or feel sorry for herself. She kept her spirits high and continued to do her best work daily. After six months of hard work, Mrs. Vaughan went to Henry Pearson and pointed out how well

Katherine was doing. Mrs. Vaughan reminded him that it was Katherine who reviewed the photographic film from the aircrafts' black boxes and plotted the data sheets. Katherine got a promotion and a raise after the meeting. As time passed, the white men in the office became friendly toward Katherine and respected her work.

We Have Lift-Off

NASA is a United States government agency that explores and researches space. Before NASA was developed in 1958, the National Advisory Committee for Aeronautics (NACA) existed to test new airplane designs and make planes much safer. From landing the first human on the moon to sending unmanned vehicles to explore Mars, NASA has launched more than a hundred missions in its long history. The headquarters of NASA is in Washington, DC, and they have several research centers all over the country. Many spacecrafts are launched from the Kennedy Space Center in Cape Canaveral, Florida, and the command control center is in Houston, Texas.

NASA headquarters

CHAPTER 6
Losing Jimmie

Katherine loved living in Newport News. The family joined a new church and met new friends, and the girls loved living in a larger city. The girls liked their new school, and different from their parents, they attended school with white children. Black and white children attending school together was only possible after the May 17, 1954, US Supreme Court Justice Earl Warren

Supreme Court Justice Earl Warren

ruling that segregation of public schools was a violation of the Fourteenth Amendment and was therefore unconstitutional.

Many white people in the country were in an uproar about Black children starting to attend schools with white children, and they no longer wanted to live in the same neighborhoods.

Regardless of racism, Katherine and Jimmie continued to teach their children to be kind and love everyone. Jimmie and Katherine were so happy when they realized they had saved enough money for their first home. They found a lot for sale at Mimosa Crescent for $1,200 and started making plans to build a three-bedroom house near their doctor's home. It was not an all-Black neighborhood like the Hampton Roads area where they were living.

The plans for their new home were put on hold when Jimmie started having headaches that increased over time. Their doctor broke the bad news that Jimmie had a brain tumor. After surgery and a short illness, Jimmie died in early December 1956. Katherine's parents and Jimmie's family came to Newport News and stayed until the end of 1956. After his death, Katherine's father sat her down and told her the shocking truth about why he didn't want her to marry Jimmie: "I saw it in his eyes," Joshua told his grieving daughter. He went on to tell her that the day he met Jimmie, he had a premonition that Jimmie would live a short life. Once again, her dad had seen what others could not see. He saw death.

In January 1957, Katherine picked herself up from her grief and turned her attention to her girls and their future. She went with them to school and asked their teachers to give them the same work as other students. After they were all settled in school, Katherine returned to work, church, and even started spending time with her sorority sisters again.

Sometimes on the weekend she would pack their things and take trips to Marion to visit Jimmie's family or to White Sulphur Springs to see her family.

Separate Is Not Equal

Back in the 1950s, across many parts of the United States, the law allowed separate facilities—like churches, water fountains, and schools—for Black and white people. The only rule was that the facilities needed to be equal between the races. However, the places designated for Black people were often run-down and broken. Many Black families were upset, but the law was not on their side. That would soon change with a famed court ruling on May 17, 1954. The parents of a Black girl named Linda Brown were fed up. Their daughter had to walk a long way to get to her school—even though there was a white school much closer to their home—and they sued the board of education in the city of Topeka, Kansas. The case made its way to the Supreme Court, the highest court in the United States that could change laws. The judges agreed that separate schools could never be equal. So the Supreme Court's decision in *Brown v. Board of Education* said that all children, no matter their skin color, should go to school together. This decision helped start the process of desegregating schools all across the United States, making sure that everyone has the same opportunities to learn and succeed. It was a big step toward making things fairer and more equal for everyone, even though many inequalities still exist.

CHAPTER 7
Making History

Sputnik 1 in orbit above Earth

On October 4, 1957, Katherine's career changed forever when the Soviet Union launched the first Earth-orbiting artificial satellite, Sputnik 1. The Soviets' 22-inch round aluminum ball weighing 183 pounds that beeped around the Earth every 98 minutes had beaten America into space. This move shattered America's plan to be the first in space.

Katherine's managers kept saying we have to do something.

Katherine was a part of that "we," and she did something.

She was about to put the Analytic Geometry of Space class she'd taken years ago to good use and help send the first man into space.

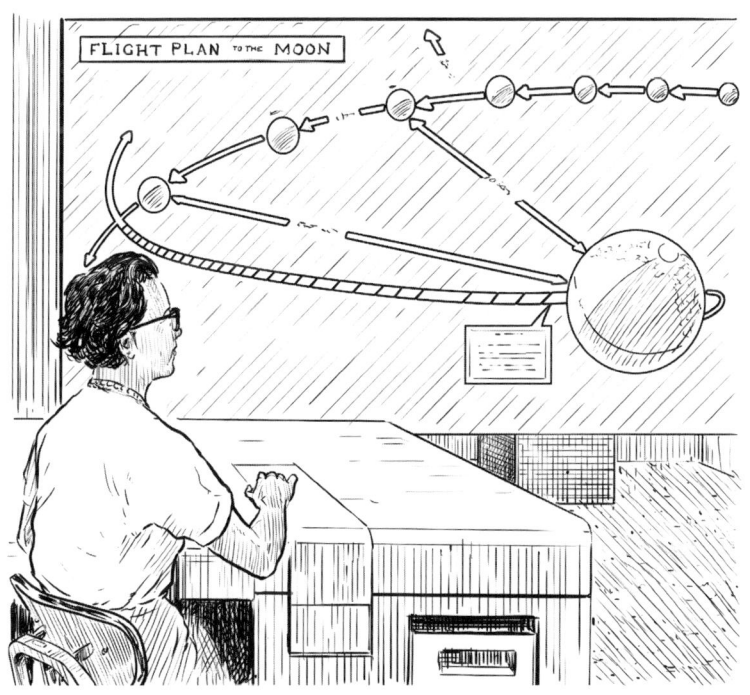

Katherine worked hard to balance the demands at work and home for proms, graduations, and basketball games. In May 1958, Jimmie and Katherine's families came back to Newport News for Joylette's graduation. They were all so proud and only wished that Jimmie were there to see his oldest daughter graduate. After graduation, Katherine's family decided to stay for a while. Katherine was keeping her promise to Jimmie to finish construction on their dream house; her father stayed to oversee construction.

They moved into their new home and were very happy but missed Jimmie.

To her own surprise, Katherine met someone she really liked at church and started dating again. James Johnson was retired from the army and worked at the United States Post Office like many other veterans did. The girls really liked James, and he married their mother in 1959.

Getting married was not the only excitement in Katherine's life.

James Johnson

On October 1, 1958, NACA became NASA, the National Aeronautics and Space Administration, and the name of the facility where Katherine worked was changed to Langley

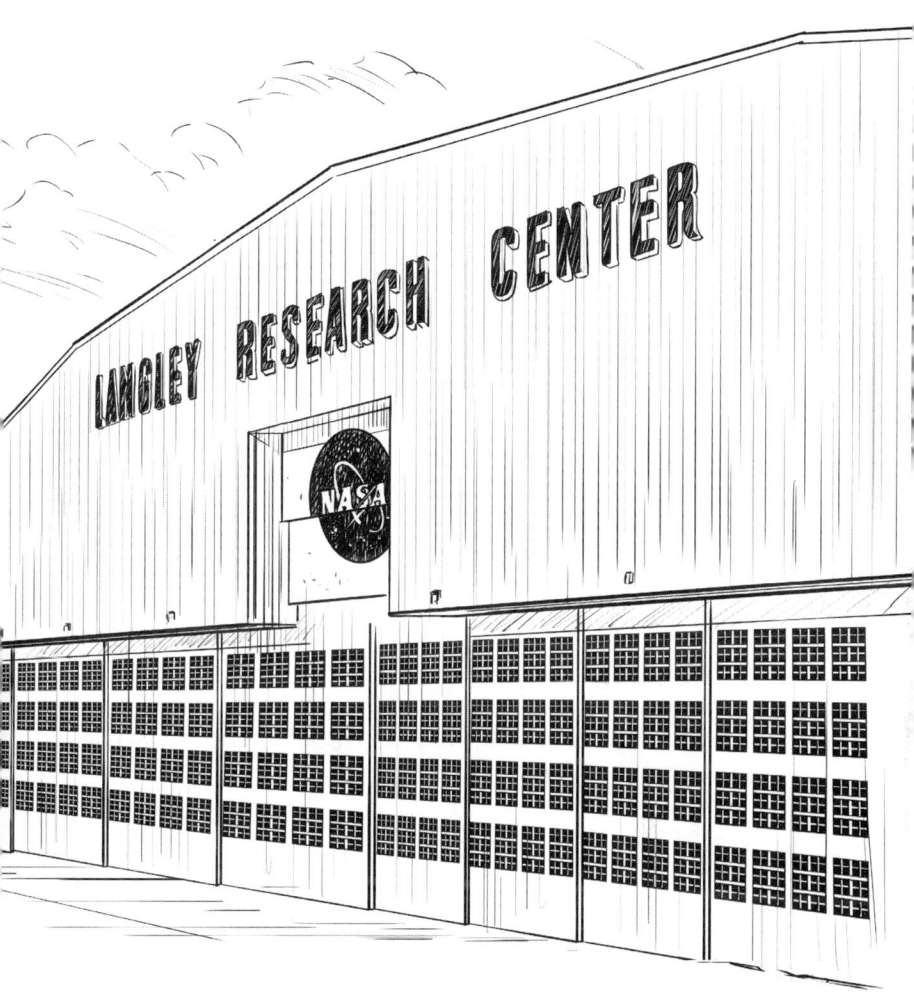

Research Center. Her job responsibility grew, and
the race to space was on under the leadership of
their new director, Robert Gilruth.

Katherine was busy at work, but she made sure she spent quality time with her husband and the girls. Joylette was doing well at Hampton University, and Kathy and Connie (who were in the same class due to their closeness in age) graduated from Carver High School in 1961.

The two sisters who were always together separated for the first time when Kathy headed off to Bennett College in Greensboro, North Carolina, and Connie was off to Hampton University, close to home.

Katherine was very worried but proud of the girls when they started joining student sit-ins at colleges near them. Sit-ins were peaceful protests that were a big part of the civil rights movement.

The next few years were filled with long hours at work as America got ready to send John Glenn into space. He was a well-prepared astronaut who checked and rechecked every aspect of the flight he was controlling.

John Glenn

He was very impressed with the Space Task Group, especially with Katherine. They called their initiative "Project Mercury." The task was to figure out the trajectory—a circular path around the planet—and then tell John where to land.

He made it clear to his staff that he wanted the trajectory that had been plotted by the powerful IBM 7090 to be checked and rechecked. This new IBM computer was supposed to replace human computers' second-by-second calculations but still had to be checked by a human.

"Get the girl to check the numbers," he told them. That girl was Katherine Johnson.

When she finished, only then would John prepare to leave.

On February 20, 1962, at 9:47 a.m. EST, with the help of Katherine, the *Friendship 7* headed into space with 135 million people watching on television.

John Glenn

NASA astronaut John Glenn was a World War II and Korean War veteran and pilot. In 1959, John was selected to be one of the first seven astronauts in the United States' space program, called the Mercury Seven. On February 20, 1962, he became the first American to orbit the Earth. His spacecraft, the *Friendship 7*, circled the planet three times! He is remembered as a brave astronaut, a dedicated politician, and a pioneer in space exploration. His adventures in space and his service to his country continue to inspire young people to dream big and work hard to achieve their goals.

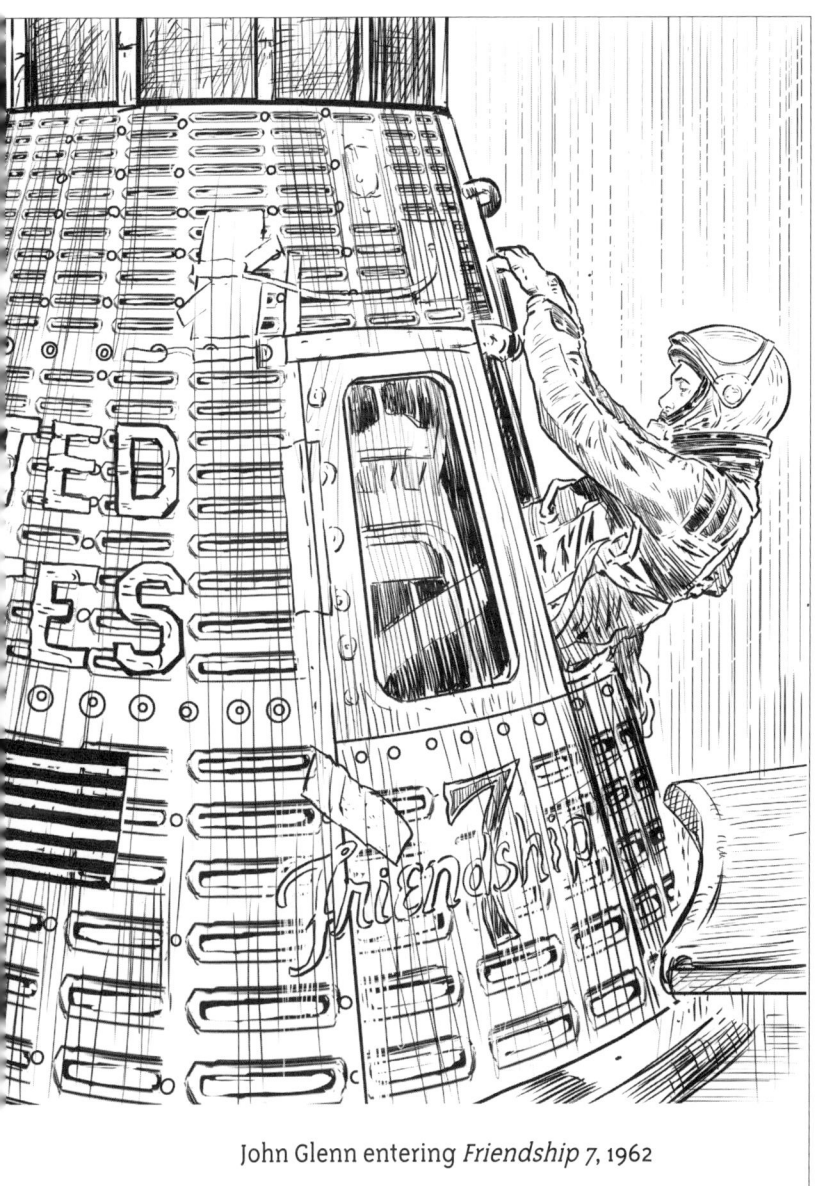

John Glenn entering *Friendship 7*, 1962

Somehow the news began to spread about Katherine's work at NASA. The white newspapers rarely mentioned her name, but Black publications like the *Pittsburgh Courier* newspaper told her story.

The Story of Katherine Johnson

Lady Mathematician Played Key Role in Glenn Space Flight

It was hard to celebrate her accomplishments as protests continued to break out around the country. In 1963, thousands of students were arrested in Birmingham, Alabama; four little girls were killed in a church bombing in the same city; and Medgar Evers was murdered in Mississippi.

Before the country could heal from a tragic spring and summer, John F. Kennedy was assassinated in Dallas, Texas.

John F. Kennedy's funeral

Katherine joined the NAACP because she wanted to do more to help end racism in America. She wanted a better future for her children and grandchildren; she doted over her first grandchild, Laurie.

Despite the triumphs and joy, there was still pain from the civil rights movement and from work. On January 27, 1967, NASA sent three men into space on *Apollo 1*. At 5:40 p.m. EST that day, the communication failed. That night they received the news that there had been a fire and all three astronauts were dead.

Apollo 1 had failed but *Apollo 11* was gearing up to finish their important mission. Katherine would once again play a role in American history when she worked with the team that sent Neil Armstrong and his crew to the moon.

Fire damage on *Apollo 1*

She sat nervously at work on July 16, 1969, at 9:32 a.m. EST, when Armstrong, Michael Collins, and Edwin "Buzz" Aldrin boarded the spacecraft. Katherine had to attend the Alpha Kappa Alpha (AKA) sorority meeting in the Pocono Mountains the weekend the astronauts were scheduled to land, so she rushed to the hotel after

the plane landed to join her friends, who were all excited. "The *Eagle* has landed," Armstrong said as the sisters of AKA jumped up and applauded. At 10:56 p.m. EST, Armstrong stepped on the moon.

It was so hard to digest what had happened, but Katherine was proud of the work she had done.

On July 24, 1969, at 12:50 p.m. EST, Armstrong splashed into the Pacific Ocean, 920 miles from Hawaii. They were home, and Katherine had made history again.

Both of Katherine's parents lived to see their daughter make these major contributions to the world. Her beloved mother died in 1971, and her father died two years later.

CHAPTER 8
A Lasting Legacy

Over the years, Katherine saw her grandchildren fall in love with math just like she did when she was young. Several of them attended Hampton University, so she remained involved in their lives, just like her own parents had been there for her and her three daughters.

One day, her grandson Troy, who was a math coach in New Jersey, invited Katherine to speak at his school. This event sparked a new passion for Katherine—she started speaking at schools all around the country, sharing her story and inspiring students. She encouraged them to study hard and aim for success. "Like what you do, and then you will do your best," she often told them.

Katherine speaks to a group of students

In 1986, after more than thirty years of hard work and dedication at NASA, Katherine retired. But even in retirement, she didn't slow down. She spent more time with her husband and her growing family, enjoying her grandchildren's achievements and adventures.

Katherine's good health allowed her to travel frequently. She visited colleges and universities, delivering inspiring speeches and encouraging young minds to pursue their dreams. She loved to remind students, "We will always have STEM with us. Some things will drop out of the public eye and will go away, but there will always be science, engineering, and technology. And there will always, always be mathematics."

Along the way there was heartbreak. Her daughter Connie, who was now a mother of three, died in 2010; Katherine remained close to Connie's children.

Like always, she pulled herself together after Connie's death and resumed her life at church, speaking at schools, and spending her golden years with James.

Her quiet life changed when her life story was made into a book and then a movie called *Hidden Figures* in 2016. She was celebrated around the world with fanfare, which was followed by an invitation to the Oscars. President Barack Obama presented her with the Medal of Freedom.

In September 2017, NASA opened a facility named in honor of Katherine Johnson.

James didn't travel much, but he loved hearing the stories about her trips when she returned home. He died on March 13, 2019.

On February 24, 2020, Katherine died at age 101.

The sign reads:

NASA

2103

Katherine G. Johnson
Computational Research Facility

1 Lindbergh Way

The Race to Space

The Space Age started in 1957 with the launch of the Soviet satellite Sputnik 1. NASA soon opened on October 1, 1958.

The Cold War rivalry between the United States and the Soviet Union lasted for decades and resulted in anti-Communist suspicions and international incidents that led the two superpowers to the brink of nuclear disaster.

Timeline of Katherine Johnson's Life

1918 — Katherine Coleman Johnson is born on August 26

1929 — Starts high school at age ten

1937 — Graduates summa cum laude from West Virginia State, with degrees in mathematics and French, at age eighteen

1939 — Marries her first husband, Jimmie Goble

1940 — Attends West Virginia University in Morgantown, West Virginia, for one year

1953 — Hired as a research mathematician and human computer at NACA

1958 — Becomes an aerospace technologist at NASA

1959 — Marries her second husband, James Johnson

1962 — Helps calculate the safe return of John Glenn, the first American astronaut to orbit Earth, in the *Freedom 7* capsule

1969 — Calculates the trajectory for the *Apollo 11* flight, the mission that put the first humans on the moon

1986 — Retires from working at NASA

2015 — Awarded the Presidential Medal of Freedom

2018 — Mattel announces a Barbie doll in Johnson's likeness with a NASA identity badge

2020 — Dies at age 101

Timeline of the World

1918 — Worldwide influenza epidemic begins, killing an estimated fifty million people

1920 — The Nineteenth Amendment is ratified in the United States, giving women the right to vote

1939 — The Second World War begins

1947 — India becomes an independent country from the British Empire

1954 — The US Supreme Court legally states that separate can never be equal and orders public schools to integrate in the case of *Brown v. Board of Education*

1961 — The Berlin Wall that divided East Germany from West Germany is built

1967 — First Super Bowl game is played between the Green Bay Packers and the Kansas City Chiefs

1970 — The first Earth Day is held in the United States

1986 — Martin Luther King Jr. Day is recognized as a national holiday for the first time

2010 — The world's first iPad is released

2014 — Malala Yousafzai, a young Pakistani activist, wins the Nobel Peace Prize

2020 — Protests against racism and racial injus' America after cases of police violence to people once again become national news

Bibliography

*Books for young readers

Fox, Margalit. "Katherine Johnson Dies at 101; Mathematician Broke Barriers at NASA." *New York Times*. July 9, 2020.

Johnson, Katherine, with Joylette Hylick and Katherine Moore. *My Remarkable Journey: A Memoir*. New York: Amistad, 2021.

"Life Story: Katherine Johnson (1918–2020)." Women and the American Story. https://wams.nyhistory.org/growth-and-turmoil/cold-war-beginnings/katherine-johnson/

Shetterly, Margot Lee. *Hidden Figures: The American Dream and the Untold Story of the Black Women Mathematicians Who Helped Win the Space Race*. New York: William Morrow, 2016.

*Shetterly, Margot Lee. *Hidden Figures: Young Readers' Edition*. New York: HarperCollins, 2016.

Websites

https://www.nasa.gov/centers-and-facilities/langley/katherine-johnson-biography/

https://www.nasa.gov/learning-resources/for-kids-and-students/who-was-katherine-johnson-grades-k-4/